THE WUG TEST

THE
WUG TEST

POEMS

JENNIFER KRONOVET

ecco

An Imprint of HarperCollins*Publishers*

HarperCollins books may be purchased for educational, business, or sales promotional use. For information please e-mail the Special Markets Department at SPsales@harpercollins.com.

FIRST EDITION

Designed by Suet Yee Chong

Library of Congress Cataloging-in-Publication Data has been applied for.

ISBN 978-0-06-256458-0

16 17 18 19 20   RRD   10 9 8 7 6 5 4 3 2 1

FOR SOLOMON AND MABEL

CONTENTS

I

There is a window of time to make language how the mind works. Words as milk so the mind survives on language.

Prove it. Take a boy who left the forest and became evidence. Victor, until twelve, knew only the sounds of rain on leaves, on rock, on dirt—no voices down the hall. No voice in the head. He entered the languaged world late and learned: to be pleasant, to remember remembering, and two phrases.

He loved milk but couldn't request it. The word was uttered only in the joy of seeing it. *Milk!* The word containing the feeling. *Oh, God!* his horrified nanny said at him until it became his song of self.

Victor is used to draw the timeline of the mind, saying we must keep one another inside our words—a boy just asking without asking for *milk*, making the world a glass we fill by speaking.

WITH THE BOY, WITH MYSELF

He has thoughts he doesn't
think about. Birds might wake him
but they don't. My thoughts
feel like speech—how one animal
makes *nature*—until I speak to him.
We use words like a tree uses light:
there is a process we don't see but do.

A kid I don't know hits another
I don't know. I say *stop stop*
to myself. Speech keeps
happening against me.
The boy wakes to cry.

LANGUAGE ACQUISITION DEVICE (LAD)

This term, proposed by Noam Chomsky, sits in the scrapyard of linguistics. It's the machinery we're born with for learning language. An organ. A facility. It's an artifact: the words we have for mind movement move with the time of the mind.

LAD: the Meaning-Making Motor, the Device of All Things Happening in Words, the Accumulating-Language Cloud, Soft Word Place Squish.

I see them, the children, processing. I can't undo the device to make them less machine. They live in the cloud of my era of speaking while living against it to be as animal as possible while still making themselves heard.

WITH THE BOY, SYSTEM

When I met the boy
he was my little organ
made to cause feeling.

Like a nerve mated
with a liver. Processing me
to make feeling

come back. I thought
there would be more
thought involved.

Rather, I became
the director of making
time between things

happening. After a meal
and before learning
to walk are the sounds

of birds. I notice them
and he notices
himself pointing.

JOHN LANGSHAW AUSTIN (1911–1960)

Austin was a philosopher and a spy. When Austin was in MI6, he is
a sentence I can't finish. It was during WWII, which is a war
finishing over and over in my mind.

Not all sentences can be evaluated as true or false, Austin noticed.
Some do things. "How to Do Things with Words." Tell me,
Austin. How? With speech acts. *I now declare you husband and wife.*
Saying what words can do gave them more measurable weight.
Like a baited fish hook—the speed of its semi-sink.

The Speech Acts of Spies is written in code inside packs of matches.
Or in my popular imagination. The verbs: *wield, carry, kill, enlist,
coerce, silence.* The sentences that did for Austin are classified. *This
file is now classified* is the perfect example of a speech act. *The Speech
Acts of Midwestern Mothers* resists in my files.

WITH THE BOY, IN THE HOUSE

The boy will raise a hand to salute you: a resistor
in the electrical system of ideas. Then the feeling
alarm. Then Formica daytime again.

I feed him while concentrating on the words
I feed him. (If I list them, we might fail.)
Then tongue to floor tongue to plastic

tongue to grit. We detect no faults
with the juices of the house. I am modern.
This isn't speaking. This is happening.

The creation of composite material. All action
greeted with unknowing. We are making
each day as if a day is a real thing.

FATHER TONGUE

Each issue of *Blade* magazine describes a man and how he came to be a person of knives. There are veins of metal in rock and in a family and in one person's diorama. Some metal is mined for weaponry, some for language. Some knives are photographed like ladies in a nudie magazine, hovering above place without a human to hold them. Their blades reflect nothing like the back of my mind when I look. *Blade* at the dining room table, in the bathroom, on the couch, throughout my striated landscape leading to leaving.

The language of knives includes: *quenching, hilt, damascus, hollow ground, skeleton handle, balisong*. "Song of Myself" has: *loveroot, souse, killing-clothes, chant of dilation, fallen architecture*. Whitman was too late to sow me as an orchard for harvesting the hybrid fruits of our thinking. I had held my father's knives and could feel how they fit him, and he was multitudes to me by being different from himself. Whitman was merely me, but different. I am still waiting for my mind to fit a language the way a knife can fit my hand. I want to wield them together to cut my past down, the opposite of screaming.

WITH THE BOY, INSIDE THE MUSEUM

A painting of horses charging
in a war. The war is subtle
but the horses aren't. Nouns,

for the boy, live in the sounds
nouns make. We don't hear
the horses, but the boy makes us.

Our war is silent as horseflesh armoring
distance. The boy's future war makes
a sound we imitate by accident.

JEAN BERKO GLEASON

Gleason developed the Wug Test in 1958:

> *This is a WUG. Now there is another one. There are two of*
> *them.*
> *There are two _____.*
> *This man ʒibs. A man who ʒibs is a _____.*

The children made the pseudowords follow the rules that happen on the edge of knowing *rule,* as she knew they would. Others believed that grown-ups merely handed down chunks of language—ice scattering into the dark after sun hits the surface. But Gleason saw through the reflective glare of children's speech to this:

> We *goed* to the park.
> He *throwed* the cup.
> In the store, we put some oranges in the basket, and then *greenages* too.

Wrong made the grammar flesh. Grammar as the right of the brain to wrong meaning into patterns. Grammar: The smell of a fourth dimension. The verb form of proliferation. The second-tallest hill.[*] The fence that became incorporated into the bark. It's resilient as I bash it against the stones. It fits us to the rules that rule what can fit as we rule them.

---

[*]   The tallest hill is Mother Tongue.

WITH THE BOY, OUTSIDE

Twigs collect
by the side of the path.

Wild flowers space
themselves. Pigeons

respond instantly to being
chased. The ground rises

to the tree. If I look
through the boy—to loss,

to a future, to else—
nothing is enough

to hold the ground
into one place.

This is your foot,
I say. But people don't

talk like that.
I watch people gather

their faces into
thoughts I can't

hear. *This is the space
between us,* I say

while waving my hands
to make the distance.

The kangaroo was in a zombie-like funk. Then an inspiring caravan of hip, divorced tycoons—each with his or her own robot to boss around—went by. The kangaroo thought, "If I ever leave the boondocks, I can become a kung fu legend with all the ketchup I need to bring me a sense of Zen."

Words travel by boat and by horse and by foot. By mail and by phone and by wire. *Kangaroo* came by boat—the first aboriginal Australian word into English—with an actual kangaroo.

Chinese: *ketchup, kung fu*. Czech: *robot*. Dutch: *boss, funk*. French: *divorce*. Japanese: *tycoon, Zen*. Kikongo: *zombie*. Persian: *caravan*. Tagalog: *boondocks*. Wolof: *hip*.

IDIOLECT

We each speak our own version—billions of languages within a language. Communication happens despite. Yet, I'm angry at many. There's a method of teaching English as a second language that is based completely on giving commands. I know you understood because you sat in the chair. The nuance of a command hides in the body as it moves. Could you please would you mind do it now stop it? Could you please keep reading?

WITH THE BOY, WITH THE BOOK

The man loves the boat.
I didn't have to make that sentence up.
It exists the way all transportation does.

He says *more go more self*
and I translate that into the talking
that's always been:

I, I, I. Thoughts grown from thoughts
are the weakest. Instead, I want
to see-talk, to un-*I* until it's all

more. I can't turn the boy
into a lesson. But I teach him:
The man loves the boat.

THE FUTURE OF WRITING IN ENGLISH

1

After being released from a concentration camp and becoming an exile in Shanghai, Charles K. Bliss invented a language of no sounds. A writing system of symbols to circumvent speech, its manipulations. Ideographic. Ideo. Idea. Ideal as the space between mind and page as silent.

In the future, English writing more and more becomes the opposite of this. Each word must be said aloud for it to appear on the screen. Seeing without saying—that's the manipulation. From voice, which has become content the way sex is the subtext. The flesh of meaning.

English adopts a notational system of dots and dashes above and between words to approximate tone, to make the speaking silently talk. We can't trust them, the words, to be the mind behind. A dot. A dash. The speech within speech.

2

In 2010 a Canadian company released the program ToneCheck, which screens emails for potentially conflict-causing language. Post-meeting anger: alert. Late-night reach/bite toward a lost lover: don't.

In Future English, the thread of feeling in each word has become an overt overture, a prioritized primal focal point. Words are color-coded according to an emotional template based on the smallest fluctuations of pulse and temperature in the tips of fingers. What do we encode into words with our bodies as we speak? There is technology for this. It's right there in red red red.

3

Dear A,

I just want to say. I have been. I think about. Now you know.

With a feeling,
Jenny

WITH THE BOY, WE MADE OURSELVES THROUGH

We made ourselves through words
for each other for years. Like trees
almost make the sky. But now—
not words—just their effect.
Acting out being a person
who is excited about dogs.

Acting out eating while
eating, touching. This sounds
much worse than it is. More like
how the car makes the road.
Or the runner across the field,
the park—I love him.

SECOND LANGUAGE INTERFERENCE

When learning a third language, one often accidentally uses the second tongue, even if it's barely rooted. In that moment of interference—there is a box that springs open. Occupied. Two spiders per web. The dark matter of conflict. There is a shifting, making space for the stranger getting onto your subway car. You are a subway car. Or the language is in you like a mind.

ENGLISH FEMALE SPEECH

Is defined through comparison. More: intensifiers, questions, positive noises uh-huh, intonational range yes, marked rhythmical stress, *you* and *we*. (From the institute of Now We Are Paying Attention, Hmmmm.)

Once passed down orally, classes in English Female Speech are now being offered at the following location: between two misnamed towns down by the old chestnut under the new warring weather systems.

Official Language of: the very last locker room of the twelfth regime of the sea change.

Today's Lesson: *to break*. Do not break the plate and say *please* at the same time. Do not break your stride for innuendos unless they will be used to fill a suburban swimming pool.

> Hypothesis: Teach the boys the language and they will cipher out the secret dirt deposits.
> Proof: Interruption.

> Hypothesis: Female Speech is highly effective at generating non-language.
> Proof: You and we.

WITH THE BOY, IN THE BOX

I drag the boy along the shore
in a box, a boy-box, a not-box.

I pause to speech-draft us a word-ship,
a ship-box, a ship, and I try to leave

spaces for weather, we-weather. I leave
spaces that are high, highly visible for us

to move into as we grow culture
with our box-myth: a box can be

a word can be a ship can be
the blank that takes us to each other.

Subject L was informally experimented upon as a child by her father. A lawyer by trade, he moonlighted as a secular Jewish Buddhist philosopher.

> Father: Imagine a cup.
>
> L: OK.
>
> F: Do you hear the word *cup* while you imagine? Are you thinking *cup*?
>
> L: Yup.
>
> F: Don't. Try to remove the word from the thing.

Subject L spent years trying to please her father by removing words from things. (The very words he had taught her.) She wrested *snow* from snow, *skin* from skin. Some words were stickier: *mother, elevator, mailbox, cereal.*

> L: Why did you teach me to take the words away?
>
> F: Because I couldn't do it myself.

At age twenty-four, Subject L was afflicted by an acute case of Hovering Language Syndrome. She felt English sitting above, not in, the world like a tacky carpet. She took her medicine of television in the afternoons and conversations at the corner store to no avail. Desperate for a cure, she decided to learn a new language—one that had hidden inside her native tongue: Yiddish.

F: Why are you learning Yiddish? That's basically a dead language.

L: Isn't English?

F: Yiddish doesn't even have a country. Where will you speak it?

Through a daily therapy of Yiddish classes, and a special focus on ingesting Yiddish idioms, Subject L slowly relearned how to see words and things united like the healed seams of small cuts.

L: Wanna hear what I learned today?

F: Sure.

L: In Yiddish, if something is really great, you can say it's from the land of itself. Like, "This is a cake from cakeland!"

F: That's the saddest thing I've ever heard.

WITH THE BOY, WITH MY FATHER

There's too much language
says my father.

I pretend to know
what he means until I do.

Today my favorite color is green
he says in the woods.

If my father were a car
he'd be my father.

At his house, the trees are still
and there is a woman.

The creek is still part mine
in how it moves away.

My father and the boy play
a song on harmonicas

together called we'll
never get older.

ON TRANSLATION: CELIA DROPKIN'S "MY HANDS" (YIDDISH)

She had emigrated to New York when she wrote my hands, and I was in New York again again looking at my hands when I typed *my hands*. She wrote two little bits of my body on the next line. She had children at this point. I typed the words in English on the next line and didn't have the boy and then did and brought *two little bits* up to the first line with *my hands*. In her time, ideas sat on different lines, but in mine—living against being shown where to rest. Is that me now or now? I decided now.

*

She wrote that hands are two little bits of my body I'm not ashamed to show, and I said that and then said *I'm never ashamed to show*. Does *not* mean *never*? No. Yes. *Never* makes the positive of the negative happen. I change my changes using the following excuses: I'm more like her now. I'm more like me now. I'm now, and she was explosively then.

*

She wrote my hands with fingers, like the branches of coral, and I typed that and then later typed *With fingers—the branches of coral* and went on shaving off the markers of distance to close the thoughts in me. I used to try to hide my strange hands, but now I want to touch everything I can.

*

She wanted to touch some things she shouldn't have. She wrote a word that was impossible to find in any Yiddish dictionary but was found in a French one. Fingers that were like the thoughts of blank question mark are now the thoughts of a *nymphomaniac*. She reached and reached outside of her tongue so her hands could reach away from her life in words. I typed *nymphomaniac* as myself and then again as myself as her and met her there reaching toward her hands.

*

My Hands

My hands, two little bits
of my body I'm never
ashamed to show. With fingers—
the branches of coral,
fingers—two nests
of white serpents,
fingers—the thoughts
of a nymphomaniac.

WITH THE BOY WHO WANTS TO SEE HIS HEART

He says the moon comes with us
when we drive at night. He says
in front of the trees behind the trees
in front of the trees behind the trees.
He says I have eyes. He says goodbye
fish. He says the moon comes
with us. The heart is a rumor
inside your heart. He says
a rumor is a man wearing a mask.

MOTHER TONGUE

Here, sky is relative to *you*, my field. Objects change distance. (You're mine.) Distance changes nothing. The snow repeats *naked* to the trees. They could care less. A day failing to change is a word as itself. *Near* is a manifesto. I want to catch one place for me that is also us. But everything is across a talking distance, is blanketed and cleared away.

WITH THE BOY, ON A WALK

A fire hydrant
in a cemetery—

observe. And then
nothing to say.

The rubber of thinking
solo so much. The primer

of your hand being
affectionate. The primate

particulars. You eat. I eat.
He eats. OK fragmented

thoughts as if I'm living in
a certain time. A manhole

has text that manifests
as a totem. The ironwork

becomes structure the way
structure should be.

He woke. I woke.
We all woke.

NEOLOGISM

Each language brings new words in differently, showing its habits. Habits—as if a language is a unified organism. *Computer.* A newish thing. In English, for centuries, the word referred to a professional human reckoning land and stars. The word moved from person toward object. A face reflected back in the screen. The lines of veins measuring time into the digital.

In Chinese, *computer* is *electric brain.* Movie is *electric shadows. Electric ladder* is an elevator. The habit of a language plugs the brain in. It thinks. We say.

Computer is originally a French word, but one Frenchman wrote in a letter to IBM that computers will do more than compute. They will order and organize. *Ordinateur.* The letter was written April 16, 1955.

The boy was also born on April 16. He shares his birthday with a French word and Tristan Tzara (1896–1963), who wrote, "I speak of the one who speaks who speaks I am alone/I am but a small noise I have several noises in me." In this sentence Tzara unorganizes words into meaning. The boy was a small noise and now is a reckoner of words. In the history of his language, *computer* coincided with his ability to control a mouse. Before *computer,* there were the sounds the animals make. Someday: *death, sex, lipstick, internet, drones.* There is no stopping them.

I compute in my brain. The distance and price to you. I don't say *compute*. (Cue machine voice.) When the French use an *ordinateur* there is the hue of organization. Of French organization. My computer proliferates. I look up *computer*. I tell the boy his electricity comes from food. I tell him you can't turn a brain off.

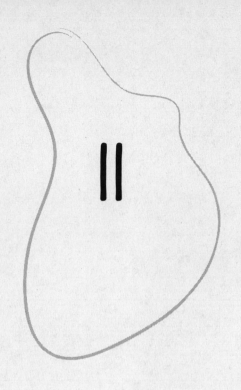

⌈
⌊

    overlap begins

She can talk and listen simultaneously. Rain inserted into the river.

⌉
⌋

    overlap ends

He stops to hear. Self + other = negativeself now. The not-him of her talking pushes the side of his idea. The right-now mossy side.

=   links different parts of one speaker's continuous utterance when there is intervening speech by another speaker

His speech, after she stops, continues on the same trajectory except with three new gravities: apple, her, rope. Its arc is the same without ever being an arc. Speech into speech—dye into skin.

-     self-interruption, halting, or stammering

The self is stuffed into oneself. And then there is feeling. It all comes out, sometimes, as nothing. And three ideas at once. Is he still listening? What happens to them when she is trying to speak? They are farther apart and closer as he guesses what she's about to say. And her idea becomes the one spectral representation. Paper stuck to a tree by wind.

. . .   a section or sentences have been left out of the transcript

I'll admit it. I've used them for their words. What's missing: the words one forgets one even said. That's what I want to believe. The dust of speech. The microcosm of that dust.

(0.0)   timed pause

Once you start counting the pauses in people's speech . . . you fall in. I mean I. In the pauses—autobiography.

(.)   untimed pause, less than .5 seconds

What can live in there? It just passed again. It was a memory of an animal moving. An unloved animal.

:   sound extension (the more, the longer the extension)

Sound can mean the whole word again if she keeps her breath going through it. Wind through the flag saying *country* over and over. When the word finally ends—its opposite. The opposite of *country* is where you live then.

.hhh   audible inhale (the more *h*'s, the longer the inhale)

> Everyone needs to breathe. Sometimes emphatically. This inhale is elderly yet her. She tastes her future in that air.

hhh   audible exhale (the more *h*'s, the longer the exhale)

> So rude—she knows—to fill space before his speech with extra breath. Like the flame in the hot air balloon—her wanting to lift it away.

.   stopping fall in tone

> Something died inside that sentence.

?   rising inflection

> But maybe not a question? But maybe you should let her know if you agree. The sky deciding to be one kind of weather for once.

!   animated tone

> She's talking about the new idea framing her. She and the frame are moving, making the language skid. Tread marks.

↑   marked rise in intonation on the word that follows

> This arrow is a metaphor itself. The word rises, points. She just talks that way, she thinks. The words are always pointing.

↓   marked fall in intonation on the word that follows

> She dropped that one. He'll have to pick it up by leaning in. Then it comes back to them as more. Exposed striations in the rock.

ABD   increased volume

> Perhaps he didn't hear what she said.

°abc° encloses speech at a decreased volume

> Perhaps she didn't want to have to say it.

<u>underline</u> emphasis

> She stands behind some phrases as if she's pushing them forward with her body. She can't trust the language to move without her extra force. The flag articulates the air.

>abc< encloses speech at a faster rate

     There's not much time left.

(abc)   encloses a description

     (Then weather: sudden rain opening the ground to
dark. The conversation moves inside.)

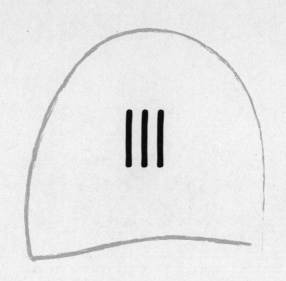

LETTER

In Korea in the 1400s a team of the king's men invented new letters to perfectly fit Korean speech, replace the script imposed by history. They designed each consonant to mark its own place and manner of articulation. Self and signal working with the resistance of air in the mouth to resist the characters that had clasped over the sounds, barbed. They made Hangul.

Every letter is an evocation before you say it. It holds time the way the sky does: obscurely yet manifest. But these letters do more— embody themselves as seen action. Muscle and the skin around it. Less tangle against the wrought road of why in the mind-mouth.

*

When I create my alphabet. That is not a thought I should have but I do. I'm married. To this script. The way you can't say *wife* and *husband* simultaneously with one tongue.

When I can't sleep, I say, in my head, the alphabet forward and backward at the same time. Canceling out what can be said to bring me into No Saying.

The letter *A/a* in English was probably once an ox. The shape is many sounds—sometimes horned, sometimes innocuous as boneless flesh. I don't wish the ox into my speech. I can only go back so far. But now: ox and ox.

I search out where sound squirms against script as proof of failure. That is my resistance to myself as speech. Instead: thinking, not thinking.

WITH THE BOY, I'M PLAIN

A feeling, a wash. I want
to be honest but stop

talking, a fist wrapped
in twine is the image

I give to keep my mouth
from embroidering.

Be plain because that
is a word. A feeling like—

no. That's it.
Just the plain of it.

If I could keep image
down: a metal bowl,

not the rock he hits
it with to make it ring.

TEN WAYS TO MOURN A DEAD LANGUAGE

1

Intersperse words from the dead language into your speech. When asked the meaning of the dead words say, *I never said that*.

2

Think of an idea or expression that can only happen in the dead tongue. Repeat it until it becomes a hole. Yell in.

3

Write dead words in sugar or salt inside food. Distribute.

4

Rename the stars with words for body parts in the dead language. Teach neighborhood children to use these names.

5

Nothing stays inside the body forever.

6

7

Use dead syntax with living words when asking for directions to places you'll never visit.

8

What is the most popular song right now? Translate it into the dead language. Then, if the song plays in your presence, hold your breath.

9

Borrow some clothes from friends. On each label write one grapheme to spell across bodies *touch me here* in the dead language.

10

Send me your address. I'll send you a letter.

BENJAMIN LEE WHORF (1897–1941)

Whorf worked in insurance, studied the causes of fires in the files: faulty wiring, lack of air spaces, a problem of materials.

Additional patterns emerged: Workers took great care around gasoline drums, but not around *empty* gas drums.

Empty: put your hand in there. Can you feel anything? When the night sky is empty there are still. When the mind is empty there are still. When drums are *empty* there are still vapors more flammable than gasoline. They are English empty—waiting for the spark.

Limestone considered safe from fire because of the *stone*. Watch it burn. *Watery* can't catch fire, but it does.

These discoveries become a metaphor about language—whip back to being language language. Language shapes experience and kaboom. We must classify so we don't swarm in the undifferentiated waters of the unsaid. Drown or the risk of fire. But when the habits of category fail: the burnt structure of *there once was speech here—faulty*. And paperwork, of course.

WITH THE BOY WHO GAZES

Gaze. A problem word
in the translations.
I don't know how—

I try to gaze out/in/toward
to teach myself how to close
a distance without words.
To slip gaze into a sentence
like a river into the past.

His gaze, once, it said me.

1

	alley	highway	path	street	trail	road
[way]	+	+	+	+	+	+
[backs of buildings]	+	-	+/-	-	-	-
[government]	-	+	+/-	+/-	+/-	+/-
[intersections]	+/-	-	-	+	-	+/-
[wilderness]	-	+/-	+/-	-	+	+/-
[made for cars]	+/-	+	-	+	-	+

[way]=the features these terms share: strips of land one can travel upon.

2

English doesn't like two words to mean the exact same thing. They become magnetized. Slowly repel each other across sentences in separate rooms in separate towns in the same tongue in different mouths. Then, they warp and alter—a fish growing to the size of its bowl. A fish changing sex when the local males have left. My path, my street, my road, my alley. I own nothing, and yet I own these phrases as traffic in my mind. They own themselves as separate via a word's talent for singularity. This is how the language owns us: by being specific and general enough to trick us into choosing a way.

ISOLATES

Someone just proved Burushaski—spoken in remote areas of Pakistan—is not an isolate, as labeled for decades. One man traced body parts to other languaged body parts and built the body back to the Balkans.

If languages carry memory like the body does—all the cells changing while the voice stays—then what I mean has been meant through fecal matter.

Burushaski was once the story of itself, but the now-lineage is no surprise to those who speak it. They felt elsewhere in their glottis. She sat in her house by the mountains and talked herself into herself as non-land and Alexander the Great. Her husband carried another past on his speaking like lichen on rock. Each sentence sucking to hold them somewhere else. But new proof can't change where you speak now, just bring you closer to that non-life.

BEFORE THE BOY, I

wove city speech
into the river.
So what.

If you lived next to a river
you wrote. That's where
words came from: having
a direction, half-sinking,
occasionally dredged.
A strip of place
that is the drowned place.

I often notice people
spitting—yes, leave it—
and right now I'm spitting
out the river I'm not.

CORPUS ANALYSIS OF JENNIFER KRONOVET'S POETRY COLLECTION *AWAYWARD*

In this book, the word *you* occurs more than *is*. *We* occurs almost twenty times more than *are*. Pronouns exist over existing itself. *She* appears more than *him*, which appears the same number of times as *less*. What are they doing? The most popular verb is *know* (yet *thinking* appears only one time). Pronouns knowing. What? Or maybe: Where? *There* is a very popular word in the text, the landscape of pronouns. *Country* is used ten times, both concrete and vague. In this book/country, there are many tokens of *rain*, *mud*, *river*—a wet *there* to *know*. The words that appear once are more defined/occasionally not real words. *Ironic* and *lie* are each used twice. *Language* and *mime* are both used four times.

These are two sentences that present themselves if you read down the list of words from most frequent to least in order.

> We are for *be*.
> This cannot like or know us.

WITH THE BOY, BY THE WINDOW

He picks language from what's given:
there's always a bird out the window.
Window-bird of language, we made you
to cry out and be said down. Every other
sound is a truck, the sound of a man
driving his truck to truck-land.

Window-bird—traipsing a curse-sky
we say in not out—cutting the swath
for saying into until the world is out out
and traipsable. I say something happened
and so it did that way. The trucks and birds
go far to where we don't so we say *here*.

Michel de Certeau said walking can be syntax. I tested this theory the summer of Alone and Heartbroken. I walked and walked, making sentences to build an interior language-city. I remade the landscape of alone-thinking into Myself Moving Through. This is how I still talk in my head.

But, then, how to go outside of myself again? In the Wing Chun style of kung fu, all motions are metaphors. You move as if you have a centerline, then do. Personal space makes a triangle if you think it that way. Your arm becomes a wing, sometimes a knife. After walking, I learned to fight, built a concept-armature quick and fluid enough to go for the throat. Now, theory allows me to hit with all my body, its full weight.

SEMANTIC ANALYSIS: BEAUTY

1

Approximately 80% of the time, beauty occurs outside.

2

Beauty appears in decreasing amounts in the following bodies of water: ocean, river, lake, pond, bath, puddle.

3

Men are 20% worse at using beauty than women.

4

Beauty and window appear in the same unit more often than beauty and any other nonhuman noun.

5

Human beauty brings the word into a lower diction than object beauty.

6

J____ is a beauty is either archaic or sarcastic, according to five people just like me.

7

You can distinguish beauty from prettiness by using a lie detector. You can distinguish beauty from pulchritude by plumbing a puddle.

8

Beauty can be the opposite of a number.

9

Beauty implies curse in some rural dialects.

10

Beauty is rarely the subject.

WITH THE BOY, NOW

Before the boy I could afford
to temper what I said into being true.

After the boy I could say one thing
and only if I said it the same way each time.

Now is the time of the boy, and I say things
to see what I mean in a voice I don't.

It's not that I haven't tried to live in my voice
like a man in a shack, but when I speak,

I leave myself to watch words
happen out there—across his face.

PHONETICS: *S*, A LOVE STORY

Her /s/ had a slight echo or whistling sound.

She brought the tip of the tongue up against the alveolar ridge, causing the rest of the tongue to curve down in her mouth.

Examples abounded in her. She was an example of herself as being from a place.

She said this /s/ when she said *sorry*, as in *I'm not sorry*.

Loss. Two *s*'s do not make the sound continue longer.

She pronounced *herself* as herself.

The tokens in the dialogues I recorded—I would mount them on the wall.

(To use *tokens* to mean something one might hang on a wall is an intentional error. I like to give in to the mistake of moving between meanings of a word.)

She didn't hear her own accent. I didn't hear the nature of this /s/ until I recorded it.

Her /s/ varied, in part, due to shifts within her interlanguage as she moved away from language A toward language me. Her variations were often sympathetic.

I believe in this /s/. That it says *S* and also something that is hissingly gone.

It is more difficult to rest the curved tongue.

BEFORE THE BOY, ONCE

Upon a time, I was
an alien. But then
I kept talking and
talking until I was
human. I keep writing
and writing to
unhinge words from
what they can't.

FRAMING IN DISCOURSE

Frame: Play
I've got you.

Frame: Argument
I've got you.

Frame: Metalinguistic
What have I got?

Frame: Apology
I've got you.

Frame: Silent
I've got you.

Q&A

It is well studied why it is developmentally important for children to ask approximately three hundred questions a day. Yet, there are few studies researching the effects of constant questioning on adult targets. Does it change the way the adult mind works? Are there benefits to these changes? I have researched these questions in a long-range qualitative study. The results, divided into subcategories of responses, follow.

1

Why in the mind is light, almost frothy. It floats in before-knowing. It expands to fit the holes all around. The answer—a small piece of sanded wood placed on the table. Wood, when filling the head, is the perfect weight to keep me looking down. I keep giving wood-mind to you to weigh you into the world of me answering.

2

Why is not a question. I know because when I answer *why*, I do not provide an answer to *why*. I answer the answerable and unasked. *Why* assumes *because* is an equal sign. Cause and effect. Before and after. Conservation of energy. No. The *why* that addresses me makes me live in *because*, a place where every answer has an equal but opposite error.

3

I know things. Cars run on gas. People transform food into energy. Grass will grow, or won't. The *how* of *why* is where I slip into a crack. It's the porous crack between bricks in a tower that has no interior. It's the crack where I think my way into a lie that is more true than I can be. Then I become a porous-person of lie-land, where you can bend a sword around its reason for being a sword. Where I bend myself around my knowing to undo answers into not talking hardly at all.

4

It's a mystery.

5

Why? How? Each question invites me into its viscous pool. I have to stay out of it. Things work. Lights turn on. The mouse lives in the holes of the walls. If I answer—I become mouse. I enter the mouse-mind. I am electricity, seeping like fire seeps from one spent log to another. That isn't actually what happens. It is. *I don't know.*

6

Why. How. I make a space, a room of thought-muscle. Here I train myself to un-logic and then re-logic. To make answers that aren't. What is a sword? *A sword is something that isn't a toy but is.* I want answers that draw in and repel—a peristalsis tunnel toward the interior. Digestion. Come closer, I'll tell you.

WITH THE BOY, IN THE GARDEN

We admire a large, wet snail
and moments later an older boy
decides to kick it. Unsticking
thing from ground—I want
to gut that moment
from the boy. And yet
that's how I define language.

REPETITION

That that that that. Content. Content. Filler. Sex does and doesn't. Sex with the same person. The space between content and content. The thoughts have already happened. Then they might happen for someone else. In the space between content and content I go inside. I take great pleasure in a person happening.

APHASIA

1

Stop in the street of all the streets and the hidden shudders there—a blank loss blanketing some saved thing's changed shape or the shape of looking in a lost street.

Another's hand on a cheek.

2

When the neighbors are all charring meat or fixing cars, she knows she lost something. It sits in her like a fish belly up. Between the winter she slept on a bed of snow and the summer she was the first girl to swim across the lake and get back. She was a good swimmer and a bad runner so what she lost wasn't lost in water, and her body isn't lost to her. But water will always seep through the walls, even when walls are the road.

She used to run down the street and back to arrive home.

WITH THE BOY, WITH FLOWERS

The flowers by the lake seem to grow
other flowers out of each bloom

but I've never looked at flowers
for words. The boy thinks the world

is a world of flowers so what can be made
into more by saying *this one, this flower.*

Once a man gave me *The Language*
of Flowers then, years later, died.

This must have happened before.
To you? If flowers could speak

my language, I wouldn't understand.
I don't understand the boy is leading me

to the lake until we near it. *Watch,*
don't, is what all his actions say.

The end of land makes you say stop
with your body as a border. Nonevent.

Horizon. There's a moment there
when the language doesn't, please.

TRIP TO SAUSSURELAND

The brochure: *Landscape of signs! Come come.*

Driving down the highway for hours: I see the leaves the way words demand: color vs. color, signifier vs. signified. I will learn to see the way words leave us: mesh of self over self. Sinew-map. Half out of control and half owned by grammar.

National fish: cutthroat trout
National sport: yodeling
National flower: repetition

In the mountain light: the tree of saying too much. *Capital hiding place of fugitive words.* I believe I can be myself here if you stay theory. Or empty.

WITH THE BOY, CUT THROUGH

Cut through.
Someday the boy
will be wordless again.
I've set myself up
to think this. I can't blame
the language. I can blame
the low river or the thin trees.
But not the sky, which can't help
being what it hides. That
is how words fail. And how
we fall into them in need.
Fill me, I want to say. So I
say it, and saying it
becomes me.

1. Basic Meaning: *IN*

The boy is in the box. The heart is in the body. The ring is in the metal bowl.

> An object is contained by another, surrounded by the borders it has to offer.

2. Engagement in an Activity is *IN*

I'm in the middle of an argument. Don't pull me into a discussion of Yiddish grammar. I'm in a knife fight. You're in a breakfast meeting.

> Activity borders me with time and place. Engage and you enter a box, a body, a bowl. A domain in the time-place of the mind. Now I can leave this behind.

3. Emotions are *IN*

There's feeling for you in my heart, reader. I've internalized your critiques. I keep my feelings inside, right? Is curiosity building in you?

> We say feelings into being contained. But sometimes— *above,* or right *through*. I lose a feeling through the border

of thought-skin: I lose myself as a body in a violence of words or reach or fuck. Organs, blood—we usually can't see you, but we still say through you things that aren't things. *IN,* you make me word-sick.

4. Thoughts are *IN*

I'm trying to get in your head, to live on in your memory. Let's tap into our knowledge. Please, ask invasive questions.

> Let's look in my head: a cut plumb line, suspension rods. Metal seeking metal. Sinking structure. Shoot an arrow to find a lost bridge. Let's cross.

5. Professional roles are *IN*

I make all the decisions in this job. I left the workforce after the boy was born. I'm drowning in paperwork.

> In a plastic bubble, I am a toy simulacrum of an impossible creature.

6. Acceptance is *IN*

I got into the class on synonyms. I see you're part of the in-crowd. This façade isn't in right now. I'm really into this new language.

I accept *IN* in, as a preposition that verbs itself into metaphor. I accept things in my holes, and I accept *IN* in the hole in my language that is where everything true enters as a lie. I'm into *IN* right now. Here is *IN*. You are in me. You are not.

WITH THE BOY, IN THE DARK

The boy is interested in black holes
because he doesn't know how to say
death death death. Just, *infinite dark*.
Event horizon. Singularity. The boy
teaches me how to mouth the absence
I won't imagine—the dark keeps going
without time so it can't hold words.
One of us will enter it. And then another.
But the boy makes an exception: rats
can escape anything, are a synonym for
what I call meaning, what you might call light.

THE SAPIR-WHORF HYPOTHESIS

The language one speaks determines the way one thinks.

Something is coming up from behind. It's her. The brain you would have had if you were you in another tongue. Your own underside of idiom, your what else, about to slip past and into the city/field.

A language just died. The way his body, moving across the field at night—that's him. Recognizing his shifting shadow like smelling bread before biting down. There was one word for that.

In some languages, time moves down, not forward. Time keeps motion for us. The other you descends while you put *one foot in front of the other*. Phrases like this proliferate distance to her like oil on the surface of saying. Behind you now, the English *what* closing in. Above—a sky of words you don't know how to say.

ACKNOWLEDGMENTS

I am grateful to the editors of the following publications where some of these poems first appeared: *American Poetry Review, Aufgabe, Best American Experimental Writing 2014* (Omnidawn), *Bomb, Boston Review, Dusie, Fence, The Literary Review, PEN Poetry Series, RealPoetik, Privacy Policy: The Anthology of Surveillance Poetics* (Black Ocean), *Touch the Donkey,* and *Witness.* Extra thanks to Above/Ground Press, which published a selection of these poems in the chapbook *Case Study: With* and produced a broadside of my work.

Thank you, Eliza Griswold, until the end of language, for selecting this book. Thanks so much to Ecco, especially Bridget Read, for transforming my words into a real thing with such wonderful care. I'm indebted to my teachers in the applied linguistics program at Columbia University Teachers College—Leslie Beebe, Frank Horowitz, and many others—who introduced me to new ways to work with words. And thank you to my family and friends—I love being in language with you. I am especially grateful to the following whose thoughts on these poems helped me immeasurably: Mary Jo Bang, Jessica Baran, Stefania Heim, Brett Fletcher Lauer, Idra Novey, Carl Phillips, and James Shea—all whose company I'm honored to keep. This book is for the kids and for you, Anthony Brosnan, who, from day one, gave me words to hold dear.

NOTES

The Wug Test was created by Jean Berko Gleason.

"Critical Period Hypothesis": My description of Victor is based on one in *How Languages Are Learned* by Patsy M. Lightbown and Nina Spada.

"The Future of Writing in English": I learned about Bliss in Arika Okrent's *In the Land of Invented Languages*.

"English Female Speech": My definition draws from a description of women's speech in English in *The Cambridge Encyclopedia of Language*.

"With the Boy, with My Father": Thanks to Jerome Rothenberg for the logic in these lines of his—"if there were locomotives to ride home on/& no jews/there would still be jews & locomotives" in *Triptych*.

"On Translation: Celia Dropkin's 'My Hands' (Yiddish)": I translated "My Hands" with Faith Jones and Samuel Solomon. The poem appears in *The Acrobat: Selected Poems of Celia Dropkin* (Tebot Bach, 2014).

"Transcript Conventions": The conventions are adapted from the Jefferson system of transcription notation.

"Benjamin Lee Whorf (1897–1941)": Whorf discusses his discoveries as an insurance analyst in "The Relation of Habitual Thought and Behavior to Language."

"Isolates": Ilija Casule is the linguist whose work on Burushaski is referenced.

"With the Boy, with Flowers": In memory of Gerard Klauder.

"Trip to Saussureland": Ferdinand de Saussure (1857–1913).

"*Metaphors We Live By: IN*": Written in adoration of the book *Metaphors We Live By* by George Lakoff and Mark Johnson.

JENNIFER KRONOVET is the author of the poetry collection *Awayward*. She cotranslated *The Acrobat*, the selected poems of experimental Yiddish writer Celia Dropkin. Under the name Jennifer Stern she cotranslated *Empty Chairs*, the poetry of Chinese writer Liu Xia. She received an MFA in creative writing and an MA in applied linguistics and recently was the writer-in-residence at Washington University in St. Louis. A native New Yorker, she's also lived in several cities in the Midwest and in China, where she studied the Wing Chun style of kung fu.